PUSHES & PULLS

Why do people migrate?

By Robert Walker

Crabtree Publishing Company
www.crabtreebooks.com

Author: Robert Walker
Project director: Ruth Owen
Designer: Elaine Wilkinson
Editors: Mark Sachner, Lynn Peppas
Proofreader: Crystal Sikkens
Editorial director: Kathy Middleton
Prepress technician: Katherine Berti
Production coordinator: Margaret Amy Salter
Consultant: Ceri Oeppen BSc, MSc, of the Sussex Centre for Migration Research

Front cover (top): Young women waiting for water supplies at a refugee camp in Chad, Africa.
Front cover (bottom left): A wagon train of American homesteaders moves across the open plains, circa 1885.
Front cover (bottom center): The Statue of Liberty in New York Harbor has been an important symbol of freedom and hope for immigrants to the United States since 1886.
Front cover (bottom right): Campaigners take part in a march for immigrant workers' rights in Los Angeles.
Back cover: Ellis Island (foreground) sits at the mouth of the Hudson River in New York Harbor. It was the point of entry to the United States for more than 12 million immigrants.
Title page: Almost two million Afghan refugees still live in Pakistan, spread out in camps and cities, as well as almost one million refugees in Iran. Here, Afghan refugees sit on trucks loaded with their belongings. They are waiting to leave their refugee camp in Peshawar, Pakistan, and return home.

Photo credits:
Alamy: Ton Koene: front cover (top); Bernie Epstein: pages 4 (bottom right), 6 (bottom), 9 (bottom), 10 (top), 12 (bottom), 13 (bottom), 18 (top); William Robinson: pages 34 (left), 40 (top)
Corbis: Arshad Arbab: pages 1, 5 (top), 26 (left), 31, 36; Nic Bothma: page 29
Getty Images: front cover (bottom left); Prakash Singh: page 14; Uriel Sinai: page 15 (bottom); Margaret Bourke-White: pages 24 (bottom), 25; Dirck Halstead: pages 26–27 (center); Dean Purcell: pages 30–31 (center); Simon Maina: pages 32, 33 (top), 35 (top), 35 (bottom); Piotr Malecki: page 38 (bottom); Robyn Beck: page 39
The Granger Collection: pages 20, 22, 23
Library of Congress: pages 3 (center left), 5 (bottom), 21 (bottom), 37 (top)
Ruby Tuesday Books Ltd: pages 7 (top), 8 (bottom), 24 (top), 28, 38 (top)
Shutterstock: front cover (bottom center, bottom right), back cover, pages 3 (left, center right, right), 4 (left), 6 (left), 7 (bottom right), 8–9 (center), 11 (top), 12 (left), 15 (top), 18 (bottom), 19, 21 (top), 36–37 (center), 40 (top), 41, 42–43
Superstock: pages 16–17
Wikipedia (public domain): pages 4 (bottom left), 7 (bottom left), 10–11 (center), 33 (bottom), 34 (bottom)

Developed & Created for Crabtree Publishing Company by Ruby Tuesday Books Ltd

Library and Archives Canada Cataloguing in Publication

Walker, Robert, 1980-
    Pushes & pulls : why do people migrate? / Robert Walker.

(Investigating human migration & settlement)
Includes index.
ISBN 978-0-7787-5183-0 (bound).--ISBN 978-0-7787-5198-4 (pbk.)

    1. Human beings--Migrations--Juvenile literature. 2. Emigration and immigration--Juvenile literature. 3. Forced migration--Juvenile literature. I. Title. II. Title: Pushes and pulls. III. Series: Investigating human migration & settlement

GN370.W34 2010   j304.8   C2009-905270-9

Library of Congress Cataloging-in-Publication Data

Walker, Robert, 1980-
  Pushes & pulls: why do people migrate? by Robert Walker.
     p. cm. -- (Investigating human migration & settlement)
  Includes index.
   ISBN 978-0-7787-5198-4 (pbk. : alk. paper) -- ISBN 978-0-7787-5183-0 (reinforced library binding : alk. paper)
  1. Human beings--Migration--Juvenile literature. 2. Emigration and immigration--Juvenile literature. 3. Forced migration--Juvenile literature. I. Title. II. Series.

  GN370.W35 2010
  304.8--dc22
                                                                        2009034886

Crabtree Publishing Company
www.crabtreebooks.com   1-800-387-7650

Printed in China/122009/CT20090915

Published in Canada
Crabtree Publishing
616 Welland Ave.
St. Catharines, ON
L2M 5V6

Published in the United States
Crabtree Publishing
PMB 59051
350 Fifth Avenue, 59th Floor
New York, New York 10118

Published in the United Kingdom
Crabtree Publishing
Maritime House
Basin Road North, Hove
BN41 1WR

Published in Australia
Crabtree Publishing
386 Mt. Alexander Rd.
Ascot Vale (Melbourne)
VIC 3032

CONTENTS

CHAPTER ONE
WHAT ARE PUSHES & PULLS?

Migration is the movement of people from one area or country to another. Around 150,000 years ago the earliest populations of modern humans began to migrate, out of Africa. Since then different people have migrated across the globe, either pulled by opportunity or pushed by circumstance.

Why Do People Migrate?

People migrate for many different reasons. Some migrate out of necessity. They may be in dreadful situations involving war, persecution, or natural or man-made disasters. Between 1845 and 1852, for example, the failure of the Irish potato crop left farmers unable to feed their families or earn a living. The potato was Ireland's main crop, and the Great Famine that came about as a result of its failure is estimated to have killed about one

▲ The Irish Memorial in Philadelphia is a dramatic depiction of the Great Famine. Cast in bronze, 35 figures tell the story from the failure of the potato crop (above left) to the arrival in the United States of the anxious immigrants (above right).

▲ In 1518, Spanish explorer and conquistador (soldier) Hernán Cortés led an expedition to Mexico. Europeans had recently discovered this land and there were rumors of great wealth to be found here. This artwork shows Cortés meeting with Montezuma II, the leader of the Aztecs, the indigenous people of Mexico, in their capital city of Tenochtitlán (modern-day Mexico City). The Spanish settled in Mexico and inflicted great cruelties on the indigenous Aztecs.

million people and forced hundreds of thousands more to leave, looking for work elsewhere. During the Great Famine, almost 500,000 Irish people migrated to the United States.

Other people migrate out of choice, often for reasons involving jobs, health, or comfort. In the United States, many retirees from northern states such as New York and Michigan migrate to the warmer climate of states such as Florida and Arizona. The growing senior communities and warm climates in southern states are a tremendous draw to older people looking to enjoy their "golden years."

These are just some of the reasons that people migrate. Whatever the cause, millions of people migrate around the world every year.

What Are Pushes and Pulls?

Push and pull factors are the driving forces behind most people's migration. A "push" is often something beyond the control of the migrant. The Irish potato famine was a push factor. Irish migrants were forced to leave their homes and country to escape starvation and poverty.

A "pull" is an incentive that draws someone to migrate. An example of a pull factor at work was Spain's exploration and colonization of the Americas in the 1500s. Spanish explorers flocked to the Americas, hungry to claim the gold and silver deposits that they had heard lay there. By the middle of the 1500s, most of modern-day Latin America—Mexico, Central America, South America, and the Caribbean—was under Spanish control, with over 400,000 Spaniards living there.

ELLIS ISLAND

For more than 60 years, Ellis Island was the gateway to America for millions of people migrating to the United States. Located at the mouth of the Hudson River between Lower Manhattan and New Jersey, the Ellis Island Immigration Station was created to help process huge numbers of immigrants.

Many immigrants had to undergo medical examinations before they were allowed entry into the United States—especially those passengers traveling third class who were generally poorer and therefore considered a higher risk for carrying disease or illness. There were many scenes in which families were devastated when some members were allowed in while others were sent back.

Today, Ellis Island is a museum and home to the American Family Immigration History Center, where people can research their ancestors' arrival in America.

▲ Between 1892 and 1954, more than 12 million immigrants passed through Ellis Island. Here, immigrants at Ellis Island, in 1907, are given an eye examination by an inspector.

5

CHAPTER TWO

EXPANSION & COLONIALISM

As a nation grows and matures, it may push out past its borders into surrounding lands. A country's increase in size and wealth inevitably results in migration of its own people and of those whose land it takes.

They Came by Sea

The Vikings, or Norse people, of Scandinavia were accomplished boatmen. When the Viking tribes began expanding, they did so by crossing vast stretches of water.

The first major Viking effort came in the year 793, when a group of Vikings from Norway made the short ocean crossing to the northeast coast of modern-day England. Once there, they attacked and pillaged a priory, or monastery, at Lindisfarne. This began a seasonal return of

▲ Viking explorer Leif Erikson is believed to be the first European to visit North America around the year 1000. Viking stories told of how Erikson sailed off-course on route to Greenland and landed in a place he called "Vinland," because of the amount of grapes growing there. Archaeologists have found evidence of a Viking settlement in L'Anse aux Meadows in Newfoundland, Canada, a place they believe matches Erikson's description of "Vinland."

▲ The waterways of Sweden, Denmark, and Norway were a natural incentive for the Norse people to hone their seafaring skills over generations. Viking ships were powered by large sails and by the men rowing. This replica Viking ship was built and then sailed from Iceland to the east coast of North America in the year 2000 to commemorate 1000 years since the voyage of Leif Erikson.

■ *Main areas of Viking settlement*

■ *Areas of exploration and temporary settlement*

the Vikings to England each year; pillaging in the summer, then returning home before winter. Meanwhile, Viking raids continued to grow along the coastlines of Europe, in countries such as Belgium, Spain, and the Netherlands. While these plundering migrations were temporary, it wasn't long before the Vikings began planning for a more permanent move into England.

The Viking Conquest and Settlement of England

In the year 865, Danish Vikings set about conquering England. Their boats landed in East Anglia (modern-day Norfolk and Suffolk), and the battles between the Vikings and Englishmen began. The fighting continued for almost 20 years with more and more groups of Danish Vikings migrating to England to join in the fight.

The Vikings' sheer numbers eventually wore down English resistance. The Vikings conquered most of northern England, where they established a capital, called Jorvic—present-day York. With the English defeated, the migration of Vikings to their new land continued to grow and eventually included the wives and children of the victorious Viking warriors.

Waves of Vikings continued their campaign through the British Isles, and, to the west, Ireland.

▲ ▶ *The isolated and wealthy priory on the Holy Island of Lindisfarne (the ruins of which can still be visited today) was very attractive to Viking raiders. Viking warriors wielding axes (as shown on the grave stone above, found at Lindisfarne) destroyed the priory. No one knows if the grave stone marks the grave of a Viking warrior, or whether the stone was carved by the local people to record the invasion.*

More Conquests, More Settlements

The Vikings next set their sights on a new island—Iceland. As the 800s drew to a close, a large Viking migration had begun to colonize the chilly land mass. Vikings were the first to settle there, so the expansion was without the bloodshed of their previous efforts in Britain and Ireland. Over the next two generations, almost 15,000 Norwegian Vikings migrated to Iceland.

The last great push for Viking expansion was into modern-day Greenland and France. By the late 1000s, resistance against Viking control in nations such as England and France was growing and they did not have the numbers needed to control their empire. Some Vikings returned home, while others became assimilated into their formerly conquered societies.

Taking by Force

Few nations have used the kind of violence and bloodshed in their expansions as did the Mongol Empire in its military migrations. By the 1200s, the Mongols were broken up into separate—often warring—nomadic tribes, moving around in an area between Lake Baikal and the Altai Mountains in present-day Mongolia. In 1206, the fierce leader Genghis Khan

▲ Around 220 BC, the Chinese Emperor Qin Shi Huang set about joining sections of early fortifications together to construct a defensive wall with watchtowers that would protect China from invasion from the north. Construction continued for many centuries. With all its many branches the Great Wall of China is about 4,500 miles (7,300 km) long.

MAP OF MONGOL EMPIRE CIRCA 1279

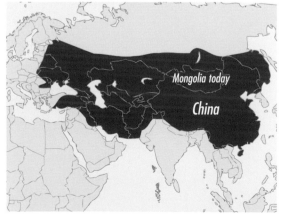

united the different tribes into one great Mongol nation. His army included almost every man in the country from age 14 to 60 who was not physically disabled. Khan was determined to use their numbers to expand his empire. The men in the Mongol army were fierce warriors, famous for being able to fire their arrows from a moving horse.

The Mongols first attacked China, the most advanced nation of the time. Khan's forces moved into the Jin Empire in northern Manchuria. From there, he broke through the Great Wall of China and on to the fortified cities of China. In 1215, his army attacked and laid claim

to the Jin capital of Peking (Beijing), one of the richest cities in all of Asia.

Many fled from the advancing Mongol horsemen. Those who remained often found themselves on the receiving end of the blades and arrows of Khan's soldiers. Even women and children weren't safe. Khan sometimes spared those he thought would help his empire—such as intellectuals, artists, and tradesmen. He was also known to take opposing soldiers who had proven themselves in battle into his own army. These "recruits" would continue on with Khan's forces to aid in further Mongol military expansion.

No Place to Run

For people migrating to avoid the Mongol advance, escape was becoming more difficult. Even after Genghis' death, his successors continued on their quest for power. Soon most of Asia and parts of the Middle East and Europe were under Mongol rule—almost all of the known world at the time! And with each conquered nation, more Mongols

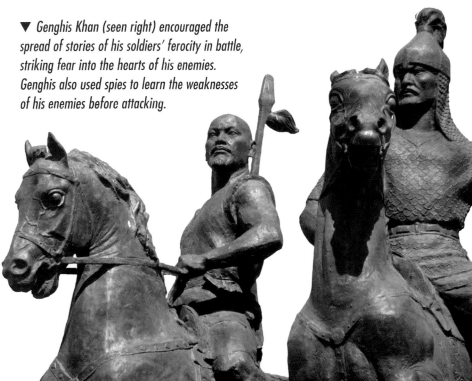

▼ Genghis Khan (seen right) encouraged the spread of stories of his soldiers' ferocity in battle, striking fear into the hearts of his enemies. Genghis also used spies to learn the weaknesses of his enemies before attacking.

FOCUS ON:

GENGHIS KHAN

Born sometime around 1162, Temujin was the son of a chief of one of the Mongol tribes (he wouldn't take the name Genghis until later, and Khan was not his family name, but a leader's title). When his father died, Temujin was too young to replace him, and so those opposed to his rule forced the young boy, his mother, and his siblings into exile, in the hopes they would perish in the hard Mongolian landscape.

Genghis wasn't about to give in. The determined boy practiced his horse riding and archery and worked to gain the favor and respect of his fellow Mongols. In 1206, he became leader of the Mongols, taking the name Genghis, meaning "ruler of all." Genghis was a brilliant military leader. He set about organizing his army into well-trained units, masters of riding and archery.

Genghis did more than just expand his empire through violent means. He was responsible for introducing his people to their first official alphabet. He also introduced many new laws. Genghis died in a riding accident in 1227. At his funeral, as a testament to his time as Khan, horses and young women were sacrificed in his honor.

had to migrate to govern the new lands. Considering the great number of countries conquered, the Mongol presence was spread relatively thin throughout its empire.

By 1276, Genghis' grandson had taken control of the rest of China.

The Mongols were soon going to learn an important lesson about conquering—that it's much easier to invade than to govern. The Mongols started to lose control of their new territories, and their military advances began losing momentum. Mongol forces were eventually driven out of Palestine, and they failed twice in trying to conquer Japan. By the 1300s, the Mongol empire was in decline, breaking up completely before the close of the century.

Setting the Stage for the British Colonies

Colonization can be a long, slow process. At first, relatively few settlers migrate, often acting as scouts of the new area, laying the framework for later when larger numbers of migrants arrive.

The Pilgrims weren't the first English settlers to migrate to the New World. More than 30 years before, English migrants made the dangerous trip across the Atlantic Ocean. They came in small numbers at first in hopes of establishing a colony in North America.

Sir Walter Raleigh sent explorers to America in 1584, where they landed in the outer islands off of what would become North Carolina.

This successful venture would help pave the way for further English colonization there. Raleigh then enlisted 100 men to build a permanent settlement and fort on one of the islands called Roanoke Island. By 1586 the settlement was abandoned, as supplies ran low and hostilities between settlers and Native Americans rose.

▲ This woodcut artwork shows the baptism of Virginia Dare in the colony of Roanoke, in America. Virginia was born in 1587, the first child born to English parents in the "New World." Eleanor Dare, Virginia's mother, was the granddaughter of John White, the only surviving member of the Roanoke colony.

10

◄ ▼ *Captain John Smith was a sailor, soldier, and writer who helped to establish the colony at Jamestown. He explored the region and his maps (as seen below center) and writings helped to encourage other settlers to come to the "New World." Captain Smith said of the new land: "Here every man may be master and owner of his owne labour and land...If he have nothing but his hands, he may...by industrie quickly grow rich."*

The "Lost Colony"

Not to be discouraged, an additional 117 men and their families migrated to Roanoke Island the following year, to build the City of Raleigh near the original settlement. Unfortunately, this settlement failed as well, but unlike the previous effort, everyone in the colony disappeared. To this day it is still a mystery as to what happened to the men and women of the second colony, which has become known as the "Lost Colony" of Roanoke.

Jamestown— A Settlement's Roots

Even with the strange circumstances surrounding the Roanoke colonists' disappearance, England again sent a group of migrants to settle in the New World. Led by Captain John Smith, 108 English settlers landed on Jamestown Island in 1607. Jamestown would become the first permanent English settlement in the Americas.

More settlers would arrive along with supplies and provisions. In 1620, around 90 young single women arrived in Jamestown. This was done to help encourage settlers to remain in the colony, as most of the other women who had migrated earlier were married with families. The Jamestown settlement would continue to grow until its abandonment at the end of the 1600s, when the colonial capital was moved from Jamestown to Williamsburg. These early English settlements were small and hard to maintain, but they helped create a landing for the thousands of European migrants that would travel to America in the coming years.

ROANOKE—THE LOST MIGRANTS

The only surviving member of Roanoke was John White. He had returned to England in 1587 to plead for more supplies for the struggling colony. He returned to Roanoke three years later with a group of privateers.

When White reached the village, he found the houses dismantled and missing, and a fence of wooden stakes built, called a palisade, with several guns inside. All the settlers and their belongings—gone.

On an entrance post, someone had carved the words CROATOAN. This was the name of a nearby island, and White assumed this was where the settlers went. Unfortunately, the privateers had to set sail for the West Indies and White had no choice but to go with them.

Attempts have been made to find out the fate of the missing settlers. None of the settlers were ever found at Croatoan Island, though there were reports of English-speaking, fair-haired Native people living there. Some believe the settlers tried returning to England and were lost at sea. Others think the settlers were killed by the Native people and their belongings taken as plunder.

▼ A tall ship similar to those used by slave traders to carry out the forced migration of millions of Africans. Below decks on a slaving ship, quarters were terribly cramped, with little or no fresh air or sunlight. Slaves remained below deck for long periods of time, chained together, with little food and no toilets.

FORCED TRANSPORTATION

Some migrations in history have taken place against the will of the migrants. The migrants, or victims, have been forced to leave their homes or countries because they have been abducted, bought, or forced into a mass transportation program.

The Horror of Forced Migrations

Most of these migrations—such as the Atlantic slave trade that provided vast numbers of slaves to the Americas and the removal of thousands of Native people from their homelands in order to provide land for white settlers—were enacted by individuals, agencies, or military personnel operating within laws that were in effect at the time.

Modern-day forced migrations—such as those caused by the trafficking of people into working situations that are equivalent to

▲ Slave traders load their chained human cargo onto a slave ship. When not squashed together in the stench and darkness below deck, slaves were often forced to "dance" on deck—a form of exercise to help ensure that the slavers' "merchandise" would stay healthy until the time of sale.

a modern form of slavery—have taken place in violation of the laws of the "host" country.

One event in recent history stands out in the numbers of people forced to leave their homes and eventually give up their lives to a government's vision of a racially and culturally "pure" society. That event, which took place in Europe at the hands of Nazi Germany during World War II, is known today as the Holocaust.

OLAUDAH EQUIANO:

Olaudah Equiano was a slave who wrote of his experiences, including the experience of life onboard a slave ship, in *The Interesting Narrative of the Life of Olaudah Equiano or Gustavus Vassa, the African:*

I became so sick and low that I was not able to eat. I now wished for the last friend, death, to relieve me. The stench of the hold was so intolerable that it was dangerous to remain there for any time...The shrieks of the women and the groans of the dying rendered the whole scene of horror almost inconceivable.

The Atlantic Slave Trade

One of history's worst examples of the forced migration of unwilling victims is the Atlantic slave trade. This resulted in the estimated removal of over 10 million Africans from their native lands. From the beginning of the 1500s into the 1800s, Africans were kidnapped to perform as unpaid labor in countries in North and South America as well as in France, the Caribbean Islands, Britain, Spain, and Portugal. It was easily the largest migration in history in which people were directly forced by others to migrate.

When slave traders from other parts of the world came to Africa looking for human cargo, some of them were able to convince African tribal leaders to give up prisoners from opposing tribes. Other unlucky people were hunted, collected, and placed on ships, never to see their homelands again. The trip from Africa to the Americas was one of the most dangerous for slaves. Known as the "middle passage" as many as four to five million slaves died during this voyage, from starvation, disease, and abuse.

From Bad to Worse

Things hardly improved for slaves once they arrived at their new home. In slaving countries throughout the Americas, African slaves were forced into the dangerous work of mining for precious metals and minerals, the back-breaking labor of tobacco and cotton plantations, and the degrading task of house servant. Homesick and crestfallen, millions of slaves would die within their first four years in the Americas.

◀ *Slaves who survived the journey to their new home and their first few years of hard work, and often brutal treatment at the hands of their new owners, might find themselves bought and sold several times at slave auctions (as seen here). They were moved around the country from owner to owner—furthering their forced migration. Often families were broken up, never to see each other again.*

Slavery in the Modern Age—Human Trafficking

The African slave trade may be in the past, but the world today faces a modern form of slavery—human trafficking. Every year, many thousands of men, women, and children are victims of this type of exploitation. Human trafficking is done to people who are frequently in desperate need of finding work or improving their lives, and it is done through deception, coercion, and threats of violence and death.

Human trafficking forces people to leave their homes and traps them into lives of forced labor or sexual exploitation. Debt bondage or bonded labor is another form of modern slavery in which a person is forced to pay off a loan with labor instead of money, often working far from their home.

Human trafficking usually involves a network of recruiters and transporters, as well as the clients who will receive their human "cargo." Factors such as organized crime, unemployment, and other financial and social hardships have allowed human trafficking to grow into a worldwide social and human-rights crisis. Counting the numbers of migrants who are trafficked is extremely difficult, however, the numbers of people being trafficked each year is likely to be in the hundreds of thousands.

People as Commodities

People can find themselves entangled in human trafficking for a variety of reasons. Often, unwitting people are lured away from their homes with promises of employment elsewhere. Others want help migrating to a country that immigration regulations prevent them from entering.

▼ Young, underaged child laborers work at a zari (embroidery) factory in New Delhi, India. The factory was raided on June 22, 2009, by the police and the Bachpan Bachao Andolan (Save the Childhood Movement) who rescued 52 bonded child laborers.

JOURNEY STORIES

MARIA:

Maria was transported by the Cadena family from Mexico to Florida. Once there, she was forced into prostitution as a way of working off the debt she owed the people who had tricked her into migrating:

Once in Florida, Abel Cadena, one of the ringleaders, told me I would be working at a brothel (house of prostitution). I told him he was mistaken and that I was going to be working in a restaurant, not a brothel. He then ordered me to work in a brothel. He said I owed him a smuggling debt of 2,200 dollars and the sooner I paid it off, the sooner I could leave.

In either case, victims may be charged a price to be transported abroad. They will then be in debt to their traffickers. A certain amount of whatever they are paid may then go toward the payment of their debt, or the debt may be paid in actual labor. In that case, the victims are forced to keep working for their traffickers until the debt is paid. Most often, the debt is constantly extended, or the victims' pay is so small as to offer little hope of ever earning their freedom. Kidnapping may also be a part of this tragic picture. Victims may be taken against their will, kept captive, and controlled by violence and intimidation.

Many victims end up doing forced labor on farms, in sweatshops (a factory or workshop where people are paid very low wages for long hours of work under poor conditions), or as domestic servants. Others find themselves forced into the sex trade. One example of sexual exploitation by human traffickers was the case of the Cadena family. Between 1996 and 1997, this group of human traffickers tricked over 20 women from Veracruz, Mexico, to come to Florida, with promises of employment opportunities. Once there, the Cadenas forced the women to become prostitutes.

International efforts are being made to combat the growing problem of human trafficking. This includes increased efforts to catch and punish human traffickers, as well as warning potential targets about the dangers.

▲ *Young women wait to be sent home. They are in a detention center in the town of Hadera in Israel. The women were brought to Israel from Eastern Europe and Russia and were sold to brothels for around $5,000 each to work as prostitutes.*

THOMAS MILBURN:

As a convict sent to Australia, Thomas Milburn experienced firsthand the horrific living conditions aboard the prison ships. In a letter home to his parents, Milburn tells of the unthinkable lengths he and other prisoners went to in order to get enough to eat:

We were scarcely allowed a sufficient quantity of (food) to keep us alive, and scarcely any water. When any of our comrades that were chained to us died, we kept it a secret as long as we could...in order to get their allowance of provision. I was chained to Humphrey Davies who died when we were about half way, and I lay beside his corpse about a week and got his allowance...

▼ *This painting is entitled* The Trail of Tears. *It was painted in 1942 by American artist Robert Lindneux. He created the work to commemorate the terrible suffering of the Cherokee people during this period in their history.*

Crime and Punishment "Down Under"

Not all forced migration in history was because of slavery. In 1591, Britain passed an act that allowed criminals the option of being removed from the country and sent to penal colonies—places where they'd serve their punishment—instead of serving their sentence in prison. By 1775, more than 40,000 criminals had been moved to North America, but this practice had to stop during the American Revolution. When the British settled Australia in 1788, this became a new place to send criminals.

In its first year as a penal colony, Australia was greeted with a convoy of 11 ships, filled with 736 prisoners, both men and women. The trip took over 200 days, with 40 of the convicts dying on route. Once ashore, the convicts were made to build their own jail. It was incredibly hard work, and there was the constant threat of starvation and attacks from Aborigines—the indigenous people of Australia.

Britain would continue the practice of forced immigration until 1868, as protests against deporting criminals grew. By then, over 160,000 male and 24,000 female prisoners had been sent to Australia. Many convicts chose to remain in Australia after the end of their sentence.

Taking Their Land

There were approximately ten million indigenous people living in the Americas by the time European settlers began arriving. By 1890, the Native population had plummeted to less than one million. Native people had no immunity against the many new diseases the settlers brought with them, and many Native people perished in conflicts with their encroaching neighbors. But this was only the beginning of problems for America's Native people.

European immigration to America was increasing steadily, and the need for more land was growing. With the Indian Removal Act of 1830, the government set its sights on taking land that was then occupied by Native people. Thousands of Native people living east of the Mississippi River were forced to migrate to lands further west. In 1838 alone, the United States government forced almost 17,000 Cherokees off of their tribal lands in Tennessee, Georgia, and North Carolina to lands in Indian Territory (present-day Oklahoma). This 800-mile (1,300-km) journey became known as the Trail of Tears.

The Trail of Tears

The Trail of Tears led the Cherokees on a six-month trek across the country. In preparation for the journey, soldiers first gathered the Cherokees and forced them into stockades. Often going without food, Cherokee men, women, and children had to wait in these makeshift jails until everyone had been collected for the journey. Some traveled by boat, while most were forced to make the journey on foot, many without proper shoes or clothing. During the difficult trip, marching through rain and snow, thousands of Cherokees died. Their rough grave sites still mark the route today.

In the years following the passing of the Indian Removal Act, over 70,000 Native people were forced to leave their lands and head to the West.

▲ *In the spring of 1943, Jewish resistance fighters, unwilling to passively accept their fate, led an uprising in the Warsaw ghetto. Several hundred resistance fighters fought against Nazi soldiers for 27 days but were ultimately unsuccessful. The ghetto was cleared and almost all its inhabitants were taken to the death camps. Here, families are rounded up by Nazi soldiers following the uprising.*

The Holocaust

Nazi Germany was responsible for perhaps the most horrific forced migration in history—the removal, relocation, and eventual murder of millions of civilians in Germany and other parts of Europe during World War II (1939–1945). Jews, Poles, gypsies, people with certain physical and mental disabilities—these and others were considered to be "inferior" or "undesirable" by the Nazis. The Nazis systematically planned and carried out first their removal from the rest of the populace and eventually their murder. Europe's Jewish population was singled out for especially brutal treatment and eventual extermination. It was the killing of six million Jews—the Nazis' so-called "final solution" to the "Jewish problem"—that has come to be known simply as the Holocaust.

Forced into Ghettos

In the years following Germany's invasion of Poland in 1939, Germany put into motion its plans to remove Jews and others from the rest of the population. People were torn from their homes, often with just the clothes on their backs, and packed into railcars and shipped hundreds, and sometimes thousands, of miles away from their homes. Many were sent to sections of cities in Nazi-occupied Poland that were walled off and turned into large ghettos, where Jews were set apart from the rest of the population. In the first year alone, almost 150,000 Austrian Jews were forced into these ghettos. The forced migration of Jews from Germany and other parts of Nazi-occupied Europe continued until the ghettos were filled with hundreds of thousands of displaced persons.

▶ *The Auschwitz concentration camp in Poland was able to hold over 100,000 prisoners, who were put to work as slave labor. The camp also housed gas chambers with the capacity to kill 2,000 people every day.*

From Concentration Camps to Death Camps

The Nazis eventually transported Jews and other "undesirables" to concentration camps, where they were forced into slave labor. Millions died as a result of starvation, exhaustion, and execution.

The next stage of the Nazis' plan for "dealing" with its enemies was even more horrible. Death camps were constructed in areas of occupied Poland. Millions of Jews, Poles, prisoners of war, gypsies, and others were herded like cattle into railway cars or marched at gunpoint across huge distances to the camps. Those who survived this ordeal were held in the camps where they either died from disease or starvation, or were put to death in gas chambers.

Germany was eventually defeated in 1945, bringing an end to World War II and to this terrible genocide. Unfortunately, the end of the war came too late for millions of people. Six million Jews, including one and a half million children, and millions more non-Jews were killed in the Holocaust.

◀ *In Miami Beach, Florida, a moving and disturbing memorial commemorates the six million Jews who were forced to leave their homes, and eventually face death in the concentration camps. Dozens of tormented figures, crafted in bronze, represent the real human stories of hope, terror, love, and bravery. The sculptor, Kenneth Treister, says of the work, "The totality of the Holocaust can not be created in stone and bronze...but I had to try. Six million moments of death cannot be understood...but we must all try."*

CHAPTER FOUR

POLITICAL, SOCIAL & RELIGIOUS MIGRATION

Our values—based on our beliefs, ideas, and practices—shape how we live our lives. These values help us decide who we are, what we do, and what kinds of people we like. They also have a tremendous impact on human migration, in both positive and negative ways.

Freedom of Religion

Religious intolerance has been a part of the human condition for as long as people have been forming their own religious and spiritual beliefs. Over the course of human history, and to this day, religious rulers and ordinary people alike have often felt that the only "true" religion is the one that they practice. In the face of this attitude, some have felt that the only way to stay true to their beliefs was to move.

In the 1600s, a group of members of the ruling Church of England were unhappy with the way their faith was being controlled. These religious dissenters felt that their church—which was a Protestant denomination—was too closely tied to the Catholic Church, and they disagreed with the restrictions placed upon their church services. The Church of England, in turn, harassed these men and women for their beliefs, imposing fines and even jail time on them.

Migrating to Start a New Life in a "New World"

Members of the Protestant group, which became known as the Pilgrims, decided the time had come to find more tolerant surroundings. They eventually set their sights on a new home for their faith—the English colonies in America.

In 1620, 102 people boarded a ship called the *Mayflower* and set off for America. Some of the travelers were migrating to seek out financial

◄ *This haunting photograph shows a young Russian, Jewish immigrant arriving at Ellis Island, New York, in 1905. Around two million Russian Jews were pushed to migrate to escape persecution by their own government beginning in the late 1800s.*

opportunities in the so-called "New World," but most of them were leaving for religious reasons. The Pilgrims established a colony in New England called Plymouth and set about carving out a place where they could live and worship freely. Illness, a shortage of supplies, and a harsh winter soon took its toll. By 1621, almost half of the Pilgrims had died.

Freedom of Religion

Despite its difficult beginnings, Plymouth continued to grow. By 1630, the population of Plymouth had grown to 180 people. By 1643, it had ballooned to almost 7,000, most of them Protestant separatists fleeing the harsh religious climate of England.

The influx of Protestants to New England was well underway—and Plymouth wasn't the only landing place. Between 1630 and 1640, in what became known as the Great Migration, almost 20,000 Protestants migrated to America, settling in New England.

Some of these settlers would eventually return to England, citing family reasons, economic hardship, or homesickness—but most stayed on, helping to shape the colonies that would grow into the present-day New England states of Maine, New Hampshire, Vermont, Massachusetts, Rhode Island, and Connecticut.

▲ The Mayflower II *is a replica of the ship that made the historic voyage from the UK to America. Visitors can explore the cramped quarters where the Pilgrims lived for over two months and the ship's hold where furniture, tools, and all the equipment needed to establish a new colony was stored during the journey.*

▶ The Mayflower *set sail from Plymouth, UK, in September of 1620. After a 66-day voyage the ship reached land at Cape Cod in November. The Pilgrims sailed on looking for a place to settle and would eventually come ashore (as shown above) and establish their new colony of Plymouth in December 1620.*

JOURNEY STORIES

MARY ANTIN:

Mary Antin was born in Russia in 1881. As a Jew, she experienced first-hand the cruelty shown to her people by the government. Mary and her family fled Russia for the United States when she was 13 years old—a trip she recorded in her autobiography, *The Promised Land*. Here she describes her family's arrival in Hamburg, Germany, where they were held in quarantine:

"Quarantine," they called it, and there was a great deal of it—two weeks of it. Two weeks within high brick walls, several hundred of us herded in half a dozen compartments, numbered compartments, sleeping in rows, like sick people in a hospital; with roll-call morning and night, and short rations three times a day; with never a sign of the free world beyond our barred windows; with anxiety and longing and homesickness in our hearts, and in our ears the unfamiliar voice of the invisible ocean, which drew and repelled us at the same time.

Not Welcome Here

When people think of a government, they may imagine a group of men and women dedicated to looking after the interests of others. Unfortunately, this isn't always the case. In 1882, the Russian czar approved a group of regulations known as the May Laws. These new regulations forbade Russian Jews from living in many cities and restricted their access to jobs and education. Jews were also forced to pay twice as many taxes as other Russians and were not allowed to lease land. For years, most of Russia's Jewish population had been confined to the Pale of Settlement, a region on Russia's western border with Germany and Austria-Hungary. The enactment of the May Laws added to the already long list of governmental slights against Russian Jews, including acts of state-encouraged violence known as pogroms.

▲ *This political cartoon, entitled* Live and Let Live in Russia, *shows an elderly Jewish man being robbed and beaten by one of Czar Alexander III's soldiers. The cartoon was drawn in 1882 by Thomas Nast, a German-American political cartoonist. Nast was an immigrant to the United States. His family left Germany when his father's political beliefs put him at odds with the German government.*

Escaping Persecution

The May Laws also increased the widespread poverty that the Russian government had inflicted on its Jewish population. Many were left with no choice but to join their brothers and sisters in the already growing number of Jews leaving Russia.

Many Russian Jews crossed the ocean to North America. Most of them left behind rural lives and found new ones in the larger cities of the United States and Canada. By 1920, about two million Jews had left their homes in Russia, with the United States claiming almost 23 percent of the world's Jewish population.

▲ In 1947 millions were on the move with no definite plans as to where they would settle. Here, a young man waits to migrate to Pakistan at the Puran Qila Muslim refugee camp in Delhi, India.

and ethnic differences, plus the fact that Pakistan's wealth and political power were centered in West Pakistan, led to most East Pakistanis feeling cut off and alienated from West Pakistan. When a devastating cyclone hit East Pakistan, killing hundreds of thousands of people, the central government was slow to come to the region's aid. On top of all this, when the political party representing Bengalis won a national election, the central government blocked its leader from office.

The government's economic and political oppression of East Pakistan led to widespread dissent and unrest in that region. The government launched a brutal and bloody crackdown on dissent, leading to the killing of hundreds of thousands of East Pakistanis by their own government. Yet another mass migration took place—this time an estimated ten million refugees, most of them Hindus, fled from East Pakistan into neighboring India. Finally, in 1971, East Pakistan broke off from Pakistan and declared itself the independent nation of Bangladesh.

Flight from War

Nothing affects the make-up of a population so completely—and terribly—as war. Throughout human history, from ancient times, to the days of the Roman Empire, to the uprooting and displacement of local populations in Europe during the two World Wars, to Darfur in contemporary Africa, untold millions have been displaced by war.

◄ In 1947, as world leaders created the nations of India and Pakistan from the single nation of India, 17.5 million people were pushed and pulled to migrate in order to find security in the nation that best represented their religious beliefs and culture.

Vietnam War— Migrations During and After

The Vietnam War (1959–1975) pitted communist North Vietnam and its communist allies against the government of South Vietnam and its allies, principally the United States. As the war escalated and dragged on through the 1960s and into the 1970s, many Vietnamese fled their homes and villages to escape the fight, much of it conducted as a brutal guerilla war.

▼ *March 26, 1975—South Vietnamese refugees flee advancing North Vietnamese communist forces in a truck piled high with people and their belongings.*

The largest migration of Vietnamese took place in the days following the end of the war. Those who had supported the losing South feared reprisals from the communist regime. Fleeing, many in small boats, almost 250,000 refugee Vietnamese hoped to find a home in countries that had either supported their government or remained neutral during the war, such as Australia, France, the United States, and Canada. The United States alone took in almost 130,000 Vietnamese.

THE DRAFT

Public opinion about the actions of the "draft resisters" or "draft dodgers" during the Vietnam War was as sharp and divided as it was about the war itself.

It seemed for the longest time that anyone involved with any dissension in the 1960s were somehow cowards or not up to the same mettle as previous generations. And while many people still don't understand who we were, at least the past decades have proved that it was the country, and the people that ran it, were the ones who were wrong.

Bill Warner, Draft Resister

To honor draft dodgers, deserters, people who brought grief to the families they left behind and anguish to those American men who took their place, is an abomination.

John Furgess, National Commander of the Veterans of Foreign Wars, in response to the designing of a statue in Canada to honor the estimated 125,000 Americans who chose to leave the United States during the Vietnam War and those Canadians who welcomed them.

◀ *Small boats packed with desperate South Vietnamese refugees approach a U.S. warship in the South China Sea. The refugees were afraid to stay in their country, which was now controlled by communist North Vietnam, and were hoping to find sanctuary in the United States.*

Draft Resistance... Or Dodging?

In the United States, many Americans protested their country's involvement in the Vietnam War. At the time, the U.S. military employed a draft, making military service compulsory for young men. To avoid fighting and to resist the draft, thousands of Americans illegally migrated to Canada, as well as in smaller numbers to other countries such as Mexico, Britain, and Sweden. Those who left the United States to resist the draft faced criminal charges if they returned home—until President Jimmy Carter granted an unconditional pardon to draft resisters in 1977. But even then, many so-called "draft dodgers" who migrated to Canada never returned—at least not permanently— to the United States, choosing to continue with the lives they had established in Canada.

MAP OF AFRICA

◀ The Darfur region of Sudan is highlighted in green.

Untold Suffering in Sudan

Sudan, in Africa, is a country torn apart by civil war. Since the late 1950s, millions of people have been on the move in this country, pushed by the need to escape the fighting and pulled by the hope of a safer life elsewhere. Many have made new lives in other parts of the world. Others have had no choice but to settle in refugee camps within Sudan, or in neighboring countries.

The population of Sudan's northern regions is mostly Muslim and ethnically Arab, as is the government, which is based in the north in the capital Khartoum. In the south, the people are from a number of different African tribal groups, and they follow a mix of Christian and Native religions. Sudan's borders were drawn up when the country became a British colony in the 1800s. The borders established by the European colonists brought together people who had little in common.

When Sudan gained independence from Britain in 1956, the people of the south wanted to run their own region, and they rebelled against the government in the north. For decades, the Sudanese government has fought with rebel forces from the south who are demanding a greater share of economic and political independence.

JOURNEY STORIES

CARBINO:

In the late 1980s, the Sudan People's Liberation Army in the south took thousands of boys from southern Sudan to Ethiopia for safety, education, or to be trained as soldiers. Carbino is Dinka (the largest ethnic group in southern Sudan). He was 11 years old when he left his village to make the 1,000-mile (1,600-km) trek to Ethiopia:

I left the rest of my family living in the village. She (Carbino's mother) was very upset, she was really crying. I told them, you take good care of yourself, and also my brothers. Have a nice time, and maybe, hopefully, I see you again.

The whole thing (the march) was maybe 2,000 to 3,000 boys. We walked for five to six hours every day. We walked at night because we were hiding from the militia. Some of the boys started having lots of nightmares. Some boys just died from diarrhea and things like that. I saw quite a lot of boys die. It was really terrifying because you think that maybe tomorrow or next month you will be like that.

I didn't know I was going to a refugee camp (the Etang refugee camp in Ethiopia). I didn't know what a refugee camp was. It was smelly, very bad. The camp was very overcrowded.

Darfur

In 2003, the toll on human life took a terrible turn when rebel forces in Darfur, a western region in Sudan, joined the fight against Sudan's government. Darfur has a population of almost six million people, living in small towns and villages and surviving through farming and herding. As one of Sudan's least-developed areas, the people there were also demanding changes and improvements for their region.

The Sudanese government refused to negotiate with the Darfur rebels, responding instead with military troops. In addition to government troops, human rights groups claim that the Sudanese government has been arming militias called the Janjaweed, translated as "devils on horseback." These forces began to attack the towns and villages of Darfur, pillaging and destroying homes, and raping and killing the people living there.

Migrating to Survive

It is estimated that since 2003, between 200,000 and 500,000 civilians have been killed in Darfur. More than 2,000 villages have been destroyed, displacing more than two million people. Over one million refugees have been forced to find shelter in refugee camps throughout Darfur. These internally displaced people have lost their homes and are left to rely on aid at camps spread out near Darfur's main towns. Almost 300,000 have fled to refugee camps in the neighboring country of Chad. Attacks by militias and Sudanese forces continue today, and there have been reports of attacks on refugees in or near the camps they have fled to.

▼ *People settled in refugee camps build homes from tree branches, sheets of plastic, or any available materials. Many families in Sudan have lived in refugee camps for decades. Many children born in Sudan's refugee camps have never known any other life.*

Afghanistan: A History of Movement

Few nations can make the unfortunate boast of having a population in an almost constant state of continuous change. For three decades, the people of Afghanistan have found themselves caught in the ever-changing tides of political, social, and religious turmoil.

In late 1979, thousands of Afghans found themselves fleeing the approach of Soviet forces entering Afghanistan in order to back a pro-Soviet faction of the Afghan government. By late in the 1980s, over a million Afghans had been killed during the Soviet occupation, and almost five million civilians had fled Afghanistan. Refugees migrated to Pakistan, Iran, and other neighboring countries. Many also made the trip to the United States, Canada, Europe, and Australia.

More Change, More Migrations

When the Soviets left in 1989, almost 1.4 million hopeful Afghans returned, believing peace had returned to their country. Unfortunately, the nation was wracked with civil war, which continued until 1996, when the Taliban took control of the government. Things failed to improve for many Afghans, as the new order began enforcing ultra-orthodox Islamic control over the populace. This clashed with the majority of fairly moderate Muslims.

Strict social changes, such as women being forbidden from working outside the home, made life hard for many Afghans. Beatings and murder became a common form of enforcement by the Taliban regime, helping to create a new migration of Afghans. By 1999, as Taliban control grew, hundreds of thousands of Afghans fled the country, again taking refuge in neighboring countries. A severe drought in the late 1990s also caused many Afghans to leave their country. Faced with such a massive flow of refugees, Pakistan and Iran closed their borders. By 2001, over 3.6 million Afghans had left their country, and an additional 375,000 were internally displaced.

▲ The Basiri family, now settled in Auckland, New Zealand, are just one of the many families who have migrated from Afghanistan to begin new lives many thousands of miles from their home country.

▶ Almost two million Afghan refugees still live in Pakistan, spread out in camps and cities, as well as almost one million refugees in Iran. Here, Afghan refugees sit on trucks loaded with their belongings. They are waiting to leave their refugee camp in Peshawar, Pakistan, and return home.

In the Wake of 9/11, More Migration

Following the terrorist attacks on the United States on September 11, 2001, the United States began what became known as its "war on terror." The campaign to root out members of Al-Qaeda, the group claiming responsibility for the attacks, and its leader, Osama bin Laden, focused on Afghanistan. With the invasion of Afghanistan by U.S., British, and other allied forces, over 100,000 Afghans were forced to flee their homes. This group of refugees managed to enter Pakistan, despite Pakistan's attempts to prevent new refugee arrivals. As battling continued, Iran erected refugee camps near its border with Afghanistan to accommodate the migratory flow.

By 2002, allied forces had brought an end to Taliban control. As a result, almost 1.8 million Afghans returned to Afghanistan from Iran and Pakistan. Almost 450,000 internally displaced Afghans also began returning from their temporary lodgings. Many chose to live in and around Kabul, Afghanistan's capital city.

Today, fighting continues between U.S.-led forces and the Taliban. While thousands of Afghans are slowly making their way home, there are still others that are leaving or have become displaced internally.

CHAPTER FIVE

ENVIRONMENTAL DISASTERS

An ideal living environment should provide us with clean air, clean water, and food. Sometimes, a change for the worse in the environment can force people to move. Whether a disaster is caused by nature or by human behavior, environmental factors play a huge role in determining where we settle and whether we have to move.

The Heavy-Handed "Push" of Drought in Africa

The continent of Africa has a long, devastating history of drought. Africa has experienced at least one major drought each decade for the last 30 years. Much of Africa's agriculture is rain fed, so when drought occurs in one region, people are forced to adapt by migrating.

As the first decade of the 2000s draws to a close, millions of Africans are threatened by drought and famine. Farmers and herders have been

▲ When drought occurs it causes food shortages. In turn, the shortage of food causes the price of food to rise. Here, a young migrant living in extreme poverty in Nairobi's Kibera slum area, in Kenya, scavenges for food on a garbage dump.

▲ Desperate women and children in Torotor village in Somalia collect water from a puddle following a rainstorm in March 2009. Most water points in the area have dried up. People are at great risk of illnesses such as diarrhea when they collect and drink water that is not clean.

forced to abandon their crops and livestock in search of food and water. Refugee camps are overwhelmed with people in need.

In Ethiopia, as many as 14 million people are having trouble finding enough food to eat—and that number is expected to rise.

Reports of fighting over water and pastureland are on the rise in northeastern Kenya. A lack of water has resulted in many people migrating from rural areas into the eastern towns of Ijara and Wajir. Other areas in Kenya, such as Marsabit, are also taking in huge numbers of internally displaced people.

In Somalia, hundreds of thousands of people have been affected by the drought. Huge numbers from rural areas are migrating to Somalia's urban centers.

FOCUS ON:

CHERNOBYL

In 1986, the Ukraine was host to one of the worst nuclear disasters in history. During the early morning hours of April 26, one of the reactors at the Chernobyl Nuclear Power Plant exploded. The resulting radioactive fallout caused the evacuation of cities and towns in a 19 mile (30 km) "exclusion zone."

The people in the city of Pripyat, just two miles (3 km) away from the accident, were the first to leave. Around 45,000 people were suddenly homeless and fleeing radioactive contamination that can cause serious illness and death to all living things. As days passed, more towns further away from Chernobyl were evacuated, adding another 130,000 to the fleeing masses—and more would follow.

A total of almost 400,000 people were displaced by the reactor explosion at Chernobyl.

Huge resettlement efforts were made to create homes for the evacuees—often in specially built apartment buildings in cities. Many people have returned to live in the exclusion zone, however. Permanent migration was not for them. They have chosen to live with the dangers of radiation in the familiar rural area where they were born, rather than live in an unfamiliar city.

◄ The abandoned town of Pripyat was home to Chernobyl workers and their families. In the aftermath of the disaster over 2,000 towns and villages were abandoned—many were bulldozed and buried in efforts to contain the contamination.

CHAPTER SIX

THE PUSH & PULL OF ECONOMICS

Economics can have an effect on human migration— pulling people toward new financial opportunities, or driving them away from financial disaster. These moves can be both regional and international.

Economic Migrations

A drop in a stock market can leave investors penniless, losing their businesses and homes. Gold and other natural resources can attract huge numbers of people to an area. If a town factory closes, the resulting "push" factor can leave hundreds, or thousands, of people left looking for work outside of their home town. The reverse trend is true when a new industry comes to an area—people will flock to it, creating a "pull" factor.

Factory Towns

With the invention of James Watt's steam engine in 1765 came the birth of the Industrial Revolution in Britain. The steam engine created more efficiently run machines. With this came a greater capacity for mass production in factories. Textiles, or woven cloth, became Britain's biggest export and created a need for more factories

◄ *A replica of James Watt's steam engine. A steam engine is a machine that converts steam pressure into a mechanical force that can be used to drive machines and equipment.*

◄ *A cotton mill chimney from the 1860s stands alongside modern apartments in Manchester, England. It is a reminder of the industrial heritage of a city that became known as "Cottonopolis," and was the international center of the cotton processing industry during the 1800s.*

that provided jobs for people. Many of the factories that started springing up across England, Scotland, and Wales were built close to supplies of coal, the natural resource that fueled the steam machinery. In turn, people began moving to be close to the factories themselves, and soon factory towns developed around the factories.

▲ This engraving shows female workers and their foreman at work in an English cotton mill in 1833.

With the approach of the 1800s, advances in farming techniques in Britain resulted in more efficient farming methods, increases in crop yields, and less reliance on manual labor. These advances created greater competition for fewer jobs in rural parts of Britain. People needed work, and the industrial factories were creating some much-needed employment. Workers began flooding into the cities from their countryside homes.

In 1751 more than 15 million people lived in Britain, most of them in rural areas of the country. By 1851, Britain's population had swelled to over 27 million, with two-thirds of the people living in the cities. By 1870, cities such as Manchester, England, and Edinburgh, Scotland, were bursting with overcrowding—1,000 people or more per square mile (2.6 sq km).

◀ As people flocked to the industrial cities, overcrowding was common with several families often sharing the smallest of dwellings. In London, the huge numbers of people were creating more waste than London's sewers, which at the time were open ditches draining into the River Thames, could deal with effectively. The so-called "Great Stink of London" in 1858 resulted in a foul, overpowering smell throughout the city!

▲ *Many different, but simple, methods were used to collect gold dust and nuggets. This illustration shows a Chinese gold miner using water to separate the mud and ore (rocks where the gold is found) from the gold.*

Gold and Rails—Not All as it Seemed

New economic opportunities can "pull" people to move great distances—even halfway across the world! With the discovery of gold in the Sierra Nevada mountains of California in 1848, stories of bountiful riches spread. People began flocking to the area, dreaming of "striking it rich." Few people traveled farther—and in greater numbers—than the Chinese.

Before the Gold Rush, the Chinese population in California was less than 50. Within four years of gold being discovered, that number rose to almost 25,000, and it continued to grow during the Rush. Most of the Chinese coming to California were males, as the trip was hard, and starting over in a new country would be even more difficult. As with many migrations, thousands of families were separated, often for many years.

Moving on to Other Dreams

Most of the Chinese had planned to get rich in the Gold Rush and then return home. Few actually achieved that dream, and as "gold fever" fizzled, tens of thousands of Chinese immigrants were looking for different work. Many embarked on a second migration, joining their fellow countrymen who were coming to America to help build the Central Pacific section of the Transcontinental Railroad from

California to Utah. Several thousand workers were also being brought in from China to assist in construction of the Canadian Pacific railway in western Canada.

The Central Pacific was looking for cheap labor to complete the railroad and had begun offering Chinese overseas the cost of travel to come there and work. More than 10,000 Chinese people were employed by Central Pacific in the late 1800s. They were paid less than white workers and were given the more dangerous jobs, such as setting explosives and scaling rock cliffs. The Chinese workers also had to endure discrimination from their white co-workers, many of whom feared or resented the Chinese because of their strong work ethic and willingness to work for less.

When the track was completed in Utah, some of the Chinese laborers settled there. Others returned to China, but most chose to settle in cities such as San Francisco and New York, sending for their families to join them in America.

As the Chinese migrants began to settle, Chinese communities grew around them. These communities became pull factors for future Chinese migrants.

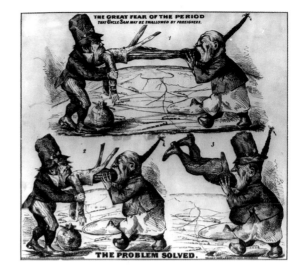

▲ This cartoon plays on the fears that many Americans felt in relation to immigrants. It shows a Chinese and Irish immigrant eating Uncle Sam! Then, the Chinese man eats the Irish man. The lines of many railroads can be seen in the background of the cartoon.

The Great Migration

With the beginning of World War I in Europe in 1914, huge numbers of white males in the U.S. labor force were called to military service. The war also greatly lessened the number of immigrants coming into the United States, from over one million in 1914 to under 200,000 in 1918. Immigrants played a large part in filling roles in the U.S. labor force, and their decline in numbers created a need for workers in the North in industries such as meat-packing, and the manufacture of steel and automobiles. In what became known as the Great Migration, 500,000 African Americans left southern states to work in northern cities such as New York, Detroit, Philadelphia, and Chicago. Some migrants found themselves earning anywhere from 50 to 100 percent more than they had in the South. As more black people moved north and settled, they would send word home telling of the employment opportunities. Having friends and family in the North motivated many other African Americans to make the trip north, helping shape the face of many modern U.S. cities as we know them today.

MAP OF 27 EUROPEAN UNION MEMBER STATES

Open Borders in Europe

The European Union (EU) is a political and economic association of European countries. As of 2009, 27 independent nations belonged to the EU, sharing in free travel and trade within the borders of member nations. Most of the EU countries also share a common currency, the euro.

Citizens of EU member countries are given tremendous freedom when it comes to choosing where they want to live and work. This has resulted in huge numbers being "pulled" to economic opportunities in other EU countries and being "pushed" from the poor financial climate of their own. Millions of workers, both skilled and unskilled, are on the move in the EU, with numbers showing a dramatic increase in regional migration.

As the EU continues to add countries with relatively low wages and living standards, the number of migrant workers to EU countries with stronger economies is growing. Most of these workers are from Eastern European countries that were once a part of the Soviet Union, such as Lithuania, Latvia, and Estonia, or were under communist rule, such as Romania, Bulgaria, and Poland, until the break-up of the Soviet Union in the early 1990s. In the United Kingdom, for example, almost 600,000 workers from eastern EU countries moved there between 2004 and 2006.

Hard Times at Home

When the economic situation sours in their native country, people are often left with no choice but to find work elsewhere. Mexico has a long history of migrants crossing the border into the United States—with and without permission. Many migrants come to work in construction, agriculture, and the service industry to work in restaurants and hotels. They are able to earn more in the United States than doing the same work at home

▶ *Polish economic migrants planning to work in the United Kingdom as bus drivers take part in a training course in Lublin, Poland. The course was set up by UK bus operators. The prospective drivers first learn how to speak English, then they take driving lessons in an old London bus that has been brought from the United Kingdom.*

▲ A ramshackle trailer park in Thermal, California, just 30 minutes from the U.S./Mexico border, is home to regularized and irregular immigrant Mexican workers. The people live here in poverty, lacking the most basic sanitary conditions, while they work in agriculture, construction, or in service jobs in wealthier neighborhoods.

in Mexico. By 2006, the number of Mexican immigrants living in the United States was more than 11 million. Most settle in the states that border Mexico—California, Arizona, New Mexico, and Texas—but today, more and more Mexican migrants are settling in other areas of the United States, particularly in the Midwest and Northeast.

Irregular Immigration—A Sore Point

While many Mexican citizens enter the United States legally, many brave dangerous routes and shady smugglers, to migrate outside of formal channels. The most widely accepted term for these migrants is irregular immigrants. Recording accurate numbers for irregular immigrants is difficult, as many are reluctant to be surveyed. In 2008, a report from the Center for Immigration Studies found that over 11 million people were living illegally within the United States. Of that total, it is estimated that almost two-thirds were from Mexico.

▲ *Death from dehydration is a danger for irregular immigrants trying to cross desert terrain. Here, people wishing to help the immigrants have left barrels of water in the desert.*

The journey of an irregular immigrant from Mexico into the United States is a dangerous one. Many routes used by immigrants are through dangerous mountain passes and across deserts. Others will try "hitching" on trains as they cross between Mexico and the United States. Death from exposure, dehydration, and other accidents is a very real risk. It is estimated that between 300 to 400 people die trying to cross into the United States in this way every year.

There is also a great financial burden for those trying to cross illegally. Some hopeful immigrants will pay thousands of dollars to "coyotes," people who specialize in smuggling people into the United States. These costs are constantly on the rise, as U.S. government efforts to stop illegal crossings increase.

Failed attempts end in apprehension by border patrol authorities. These immigrants are detained and sent back home or held in the United States for trial—losing the money they have paid to the "coyotes." For those who do make it across, there is the risk of being exploited by potential employers who pay irregular immigrant workers considerably less than they would a U.S. citizen.

▶ *An irregular migrant rides* El Tren de Muerte *(The Death Train) through Mexico and over the U.S. border toward* El Norte *(The North) as America is known. Many migrants will fall off, be sucked under the train and crushed.*

JOURNEY STORIES

TOMAS:

Here is how one young Mexican, named Tomas, described the harrowing experience of riding beneath a train to get into the United States from Mexico:

The way it works is that you have to make your way to Ciudad Acuna, which is the border town across from Del Rio, Texas, and you wait around until the northbound train stops—which it's going to do for about two minutes, and that's all the time you have to scramble underneath the train. . . The truth is, once the train starts to move and sparks start to fly off the tracks and the wheels kick pebbles up at you, you could really lose it. . . What's dangerous is if you get scared or inattentive, and that's when you can fall down under the wheels and get your feet cut off or worse.

Differing Views On the Economic Impact of Irregular Migrant Workers

The debate on irregular immigrants is ongoing. Many U.S. citizens argue that these migrants are criminals who skirt immigration laws. Others argue that irregular immigrants place an added burden on health and other social services. Immigrants also take jobs that could be filled by U.S. citizens. Many opposed to irregular immigration want to see an increase in border security, as well as stricter legislation against businesses that hire irregular immigrants.

On the other hand, irregular immigrants make important contributions in the United States. If the United States were to suddenly lose its irregular immigrants, 5 percent of the workforce, or roughly 7.2 million jobs, would become vacant. While it seems as if this would instantly benefit unemployed U.S. citizens, not all of these open jobs are desirable, and many would go unfilled. Irregular immigrants make up a considerable part of the U.S. workforce. They are generally hard workers who want to please their employers, and they take jobs in the service and construction industries that many native-born citizens don't want.

◄ *Protestors campaigning for rights and help for irregular immigrant workers carry banners that read, IMMIGRANTS ARE AMERICA. In a world where so many of us have migration in our history, the debate about immigration, illegal or legal, will continue to go on.*

The Pros and Cons of Migration

There are always pros and cons to any migration situation. For example, when workers migrate, a shortage of labor in their home country may follow. The same goes for doctors, nurses,

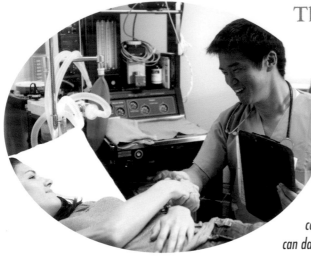

◀ In the United States, Canada, the UK, and New Zealand over 25% of medical professionals are immigrants. The migration of health workers can have positive and negative effects on their home country. The money sent home can help alleviate poverty, and when workers return they may bring new skills back to their country. On the negative side, the loss of trained medical professionals can damage the healthcare system of the country they came from.

lawyers, scientists, trades people, and other skilled workers. Known as a "Brain Drain," the loss of these skilled and technical people can hurt a nation economically as well as in terms of social, medical, and scientific advancement. In the receiving country, however, migrants provide bodies for a work force, often filling roles in farming, factories, transportation, and the service industry. In the United States, for example, there are many jobs in the service sector that natural-born Americans don't want to do. These include many jobs involved with caring for the elderly, a market that by 2050 will need more than five million workers.

Nations such as Canada and the United States have benefitted greatly from the immigration of skilled people from other countries. A shortage of healthcare professionals in the 1960s saw the United States looking beyond its borders. Between 1965 and 1974 almost 75,000 foreign physicians migrated to the United States.

In a receiving country the arrival of migrants, particularly in large numbers, may cause the social and public services of a region to become severely strained. On the positive side, immigrants to North America earn hundreds of billions of dollars each year and in turn pay billions of dollars in taxes.

For the migrant workers the negatives may be that they find themselves being paid less than local- or native-born workers. Also, depending on how they are paid, irregular immigrants in the United States may

▲ Today, cities such as Los Angeles, New York, London, and Toronto, are made up of a rich and diverse mixing of people and their foods, entertainment, art, sports, and languages. Celebrations, such as Chinese New Year and the Chinese lantern festival, are not only celebrated by immigrant Chinese communities, but are enjoyed by all the residents of a city wherever their origins lie.

pay taxes on their earnings, but will not be able to collect social security, which is what the government pays its citizens when they retire. On the positive side, migrant workers are able to send money home to their families. Known as remittances, this money can greatly benefit the economy of the migrant's home country.

Economic factors aside, one must also consider the cultural benefits of migration. With more people of different racial and ethnic groups moving to an area, the culture of that area is greatly enhanced.

GLOSSARY

abolitionism A movement aimed toward ending the practice or institution of slavery

communist A person who believes in a system in which the government owns all the property and makes all economic decisions; can also refer to a political party, a person belonging to that party, or a system that is based on these beliefs

contamination Making something impure by exposure to pollutants or other dangerous substances

czar An emperor of Russia before the Russian Revolution in 1917

dissent To oppose the official policies of a state

dissenter Someone who opposes official policies of a state

draft Required service in the military

exodus A mass departure of people

faction A small, organized group that disagrees with the larger group they belong to

fallout Radioactive particles that are sent into the atmosphere after a nuclear explosion and that then fall to Earth

forced labor The condition in which people are made to work without pay

gas chamber An airtight room that can be filled with poisonous gas as a means of execution

ghetto A part of a city set aside as a place for a minority population, often living in crowded or poor conditions

Gold Rush A period of rapid migration to an area where deposits of gold have been discovered

guerilla warfare War conducted by fighters who belong to small, independent groups; usually fought against larger government forces. Guerilla forces are often described as "irregular," while government forces are usually described as "regular"

Holocaust The mass murder of millions of Jews by Nazi Germany during World War II

immunity The body's natural resistance to an illness

44

indigenous Native to or originating from a particular place, usually at or near where it is found

influx The arrival of a large number of people

internally displaced When a person has been forced to leave their home to avoid the effects of war, persecution, or natural or human-made disasters, and that person is still inside their own country

lynching The murder of someone by a mob, usually by hanging

partitioned When something is divided into separate parts; in the case of a country, when it is divided into separate nations

persecution The inflicting of pain, suffering, or harm on someone, especially for reasons of racial, religious, or ethnic background

pillage To take goods from someone by force

pogrom An organized attack, often by the government using military troops, against a specific group

privateer A ship that is armed and staffed privately, but hired to serve as part of a government or military force; can also refer to a crew member or commander of a privateer

refugee A person who has been forced to leave his or her own country, usually to escape war, poverty, or persecution

subhuman (of behavior or character) Considered unworthy of being considered human

Taliban A Sunni Islamist religious and political group that governed Afghanistan from 1996 to 2001. It has become a strong insurgency movement fighting a guerilla war against the current government of Afghanistan and allied forces

Underground Railroad A system of secret routes used to help slaves escape from the South to the North and to Canada during the years leading up to the Civil War. Escaped slaves and their helpers traveled along a loose network of roadways, trails, and paths connecting houses and other buildings, known as "stations," along the way

Vikings Scandinavian warriors and traders who raided and settled portions of northern Europe and Greenland

IDEAS FOR DISCUSSION

- Ask your parents or other important adults in your life about their family history. Did their family come from somewhere else? Try to trace their history and see what different countries and regions you can identify.

- Find out what cultures have influenced the area where you live. Where did people belonging to those cultures come from? What brought them here? Using what you have learned about the conditions that affect human migration, describe whether you think the reasons they migrated were based primarily on "push" or "pull" factors.

- With your friends or classmates, talk about what you would have done if you were in the same situations as some of the groups mentioned in this book. Would you have migrated? Where would you have gone? Do you think you'd want to return to where you had come from?

- Have you or your family or friends ever talked about migrating to another part of the country—or even to another part of the world? What are some of the factors that might be behind such a move?

FURTHER INFORMATION

www.ellisisland.org
Read about a variety of subjects related to human migration, immigration, and tracing one's family background on the official Web site for Ellis Island. Use the "Passenger Search" link to search for arrival records at Ellis Island. See if you can find people with any of your family names!

www.iom.int
The International Organization for Migration (IOM) works with governments, and other groups to promote "humane and orderly migration for the benefit of all." The IOM provides services to governments and migrants in pursuit of this aim. Here you can learn about the different services available to people looking to migrate.

www.un.org/esa/population/migration
The International Migration and Development division of the United Nations is devoted to providing information about international migration. Check out the links in the "Data" group to find numbers of migrants in different places around the world.

www.buzzle.com/articles/world-cultures-heritage
Read articles, stories, and accounts of hundreds of events and phenomena in world culture and heritage on this remarkable Web site.

INDEX

INDEX

ABOUT THE AUTHOR

Robert Walker has written for newspapers and magazines across the country and is the author of several books for young readers. Robert lives with his wife Deanna in the small town of Ridgeway with their small dog, Spaghetti.